DO
DISRUPT

**Change the status quo.
Or become it.**

Mark Shayler

Published by
The Do Book Company 2013
Works in Progress Publishing Ltd
www.thedobook.co

Text & Illustrations copyright
© Mark Shayler 2013

A CIP catalogue record for this book is
available from the British Library

ISBN 978-1-907974-04-5

3 5 7 9 10 8 6 4

To find out more about our company,
books and authors, please visit
www.thedobook.co

5% of our proceeds from the sale
of this book is given to The Do
Lectures to help it achieve its aim
of making positive change:
www.thedolectures.com

Cover design by James Victore
Inside design by Anthony Oram - Hold

Made in Britain

Printed on Naturalis an FSC-certified
paper made in Scotland

Printed and bound in Wales
by Gomer Press Ltd

This book is dedicated to Nicola.
Ying to my Yang.
Squire to my Brown.
Egg to my bacon.
Gin to my tonic.
Paul to my John.
Ernie to my Eric.
Dandelion to my Burdock.
Vic to my Bob.
Marr to my Morrisey.
Love and Peace x

Contents

IF IT AIN'T BROKE.

BREAK IT.

Tom Peters

Henry Ford

IF YOU ALWAYS DO WHAT YOU'VE ALWAYS DONE YOU'LL ALWAYS GET WHAT YOU ALWAYS GOT.

THIS BOOK IS ABOUT DISRUPTION.

It's about doing things differently. About having ideas that will change the world. That will at least change your world. It's also about delivering those ideas.

Having ideas is easy. The difficulty is making them work. The block can be confidence; befuddlement; inertia; money; knowing where to start. It's easy to say but you just need to start.

This workbook will help you create ideas and it will help you take those ideas from concept to customer. It'll help you do things differently. Hopefully it will make you happy.

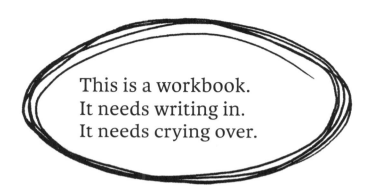

This is a workbook.
It needs writing in.
It needs crying over.

Isak Dinesen got it right:

THE CURE FOR ANYTHING IS SALT WATER: SWEAT, TEARS OR THE SEA

So, write your name here :

– –

And draw a picture of yourself here :

Don't be shy – it doesn't have to be a good drawing. A stick person will do. Sometimes we forget to draw (as we forget to play), and this is part of creating, of communicating, of telling your story. So pick up a pencil, stick your tongue out the side of your mouth, concentrate and draw.

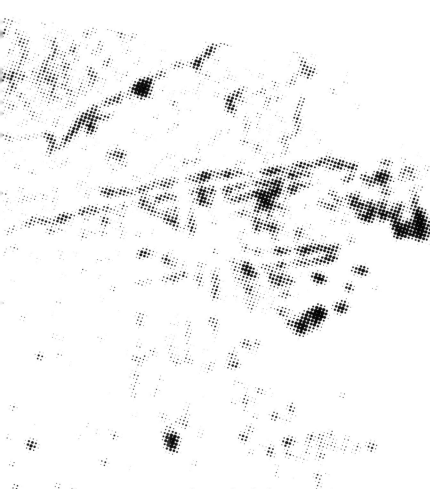

(In case you run out of space for the last exercise, or any of the others that follow, you can use the Notes pages at the back of this book to doodle, draw and write extra stuff).

1.
CHANGE

Why do you need to disrupt anything?

Aren't things going swimmingly?

My guess is that you're reading this because you're not happy. Maybe a little 'not happy'. Maybe a lot 'not happy'. The first and most important step is realising that you're not as happy as you could be. The second is believing that you can change things...

                    ...if you want to.

Are you happy?

Yes

No

change Something

do you want to be happy?

Yes

No

Keep doing the same thing

WHAT?

Surely everyone wants to be happy, right?

Not necessarily.

I know lots of people who aren't happy. Who've been telling me they're not happy, for months. Even years. But they've not done anything about it. So what do I conclude from this? That they are happy being unhappy? That they like the role of moaner in their group of friends?

No, that would be crazy. Wouldn't it? Think about it. How many people do you know that seem to like being unhappy? The thing is, being unhappy can be easier than changing things to be happy.

Maybe you're fed up with working for 'the man'.

I worked for 'the man' once.

I won't make that mistake again.

THE MAN

Maybe your ethics don't match your employer's. This is a problem. Your purpose, your moral compass, your beliefs are important. Compromising them makes you unhappy. It's important to do the right things.

IT'S NOT SUFFICIENT TO DO THINGS BETTER, WE NEED TO DO BETTER THINGS.

Me, Mark Shayler.

There's a couple of simple tests here. Think about what you do. Explain it in one sentence.

Write it down here :

Now, what would the 20-year-old you – the possibly naïve, perhaps foolish you, but the essence of you – what would that you make of what you do now?

Honestly. Imagine the conversation. How would it go?

Would you be a disappointment to your younger self?

Here's the 20-year-old me.

The young me would be OK with what I'm doing now but would definitely not have been OK with some of the people I've worked for and the work I've done. This guide from your past will help you move forwards.

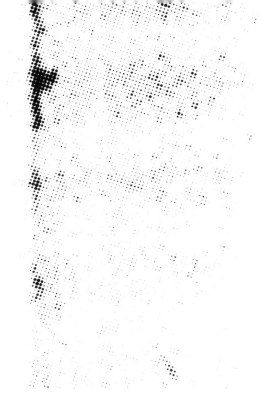

Some of you may be too close to 20, may even be under 20. Hey, that's not a problem. Use your old mentors – use your grandparents. Think, what would they say about what you do? Would it make them proud?

Here's my Nan and Pap.

Older people often have a different perspective. They know that being famous for selling computers isn't important, and that doing great things and the quality of your relationships are. Proximity to death brings great clarity.

And here's the thing.

We don't know when that will be.

So perhaps we need a quick word about the right time to start.

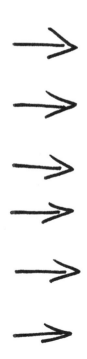

THERE IS ONLY ONE TIME.

Here's a little exercise
to underline why.

Take a one-metre tape measure.

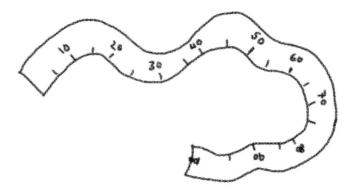

Cut it at your age – for me it's 44.

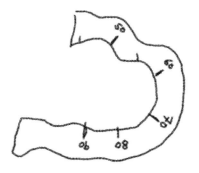

And again at your likely death age
(family history will help you here).
Scary, huh?

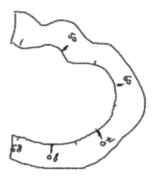

And again at when you expect
to retire. *

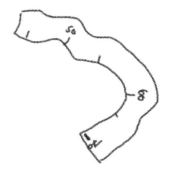

* I've got four kids, I may never retire.

So that's what I've got left.

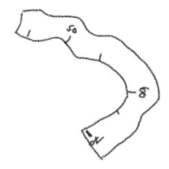

And I'll spend a third of this time sleeping.

BETTER GET CRACKING THEN.

You'll only regret the things that you don't do.

PEOPLE SAY TIME EQUALS MONEY.

THEY'RE WRONG.

IT'S MUCH MORE IMPORTANT THAN THAT.

As Jessie J says, 'It's not about the money.'

If you were solely interested in money you wouldn't be reading this. Money is important. We all need to live and we all need to earn. But earning it the right way is important.

Mickey Smith (a Do Lectures speaker from 2011) says in his film 'Dark side of the Lens':

© Do Lectures 2011

'IF I CAN ONLY SCRAPE A LIVING, AT LEAST IT WILL BE A LIVING WORTH SCRAPING.'

These words haunt me. This sense of worth, of purpose, of value is missing from many lives. Time to change that.

Of course you may not want to change the world. That may not be your bag. And that's cool (but its getting warmer).

It might be that you're just bored doing what you do. So you need to change it.

Or you may love what you do and who you do it for. But you want to do something great in that role. Or you may be returning to work but don't fancy a job. Or you may have 'retired' and don't want to retire. As The Enemy say 'I'm sick, sick, sick and tired of working just to be retired.'

So don't.

DO SOMETHING YOU LOVE.

The key thing is that you want to change something, to make it better. Write down what you want to change and why in the box below.

Elvis didn't want to be a singer. He wanted to change music. If you're going to have a dream, have a bloody big one. We all have a little Elvis in us. Time to let him out.

Try and let out the pre-Las Vegas Elvis, less deep-fat frying involved.

2.
DISRUPT

WHY DISRUPT?

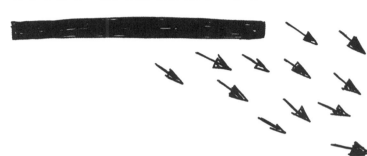

Why not shake ever so gently?

The thing with shaking gently is that you will only get gentle change. Disruptors win. Companies that change markets boom. Great leaps forward come from big external kicks to the market. There are loads of examples of companies who forgot to disrupt, to innovate. Companies that saw their markets disappear. Overnight.

SONY MISSED THE MP3.

Coke and Pepsi missed energy drinks.
Hoover missed cyclone technology.
Kodak missed digital.
Nokia forgot about innovation.
Travel agents didn't see t'internet.
Decca missed the Beatles.
Borders missed ebooks.

Large organisations are not able to disrupt.

Or rather they don't dare to. They have too much to lose. When you have nothing you have nothing to lose, hence smaller and younger businesses are much better placed to disrupt. Even pressure groups (usually very disruptive) suffer from this. Once Greenpeace became really successful they took fewer risks. They had too much to lose. They had money and therefore were worth suing if they were too disruptive. They also had a lot of supporters (like share-holders really) that they didn't want to offend. So growing bigger pushes organisations into the middle of the road.

The middle of the road is no place to be from a road safety, music, creative or fashion point of view.

CHANGE HAPPENS AT THE EDGES.

THIS HAPPENS
WITH BANDS.

They start off all rebellious, all cocky, a bit naïve, a bit excitable. They write their first LP in this state. They write their second whilst in hotel room touring the first LP. They write their third when they are rich and have lost their hunger. That's why the best bands break up after the first album and why the Rolling Stones should have stopped years ago. But hang on, hold your horses. What about the Beatles?

Some of their best work came later (Revolver is a particular favourite of mine). There will always be bands (or organisations) that continue to innovate. The secret is that they ensure they've got fresh stimuli: new people, ideas and even 'meditation' to push things on.

Large companies know this so they employ agencies to be 'hungry' for them or they buy up small hungry companies who change things. That's why Colgate bought Toms of Maine, Coca Cola bought Innocent, Unilever bought Ben and Jerrys, Cadburys bought Green and Blacks, Timberland bought Howies and Avis bought Zip Car.

If they can't be disruptive then they buy someone that is. The irony here is that these small disruptive companies have generally stopped being disruptive by then.

SO, YOU NEED TO DISRUPT.

➡ You need to think.
Thinking is good.
Ideas are what make us tick
(and tock).

Good ideas make your heart beat faster (boom) and take all
the air out of the room. So you need ideas. But having the
idea is the easiest thing. I invented hard disc recorders for
video in 1987. I just had no way of making them. An idea is
nothing without delivery.

So this book will help you make your ideas real. The thing is you can already do this, you just need a hand to hold (choose the left one).

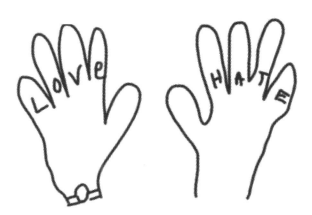

YOU'LL HAVE TO DO SOME WORK TOO.

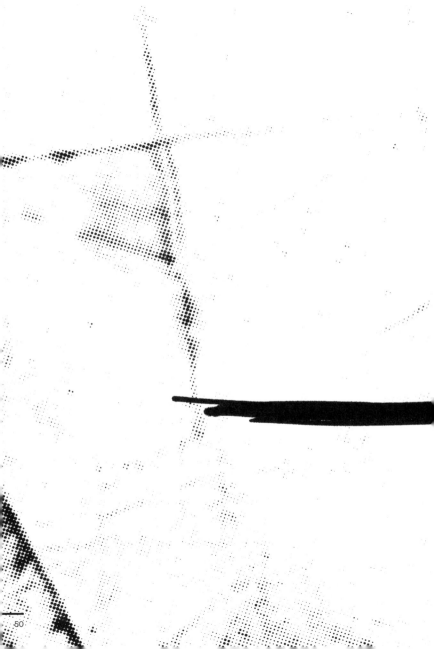

3.
THE
BIG
IDEA

SO WHAT'S YOUR IDEA THEN

Maybe you've not got one yet. The first exercise looks at what you love to do. If you already have an idea stay with me for a bit longer, it won't hurt to go over this stuff. When you turn the page over, you'll see three columns with titles:

Things you like doing
Things you care about
Things you are good at

Spend some time filling them in.
Be honest, you're defining your purpose here.

Things you are good at

Things you care about

Things you like doing

So you've listed your passions, your skills and the things that give you pleasure. Now I want you to spend a half-hour thinking about how these could all come together. Think about some crazy stuff and some boring stuff then list them on the next page.

MY BIG LIST OF POSSIBLE IDEAS

Was that OK? Too difficult? A bit forced? OK that's cool. This next exercise might help. Follow the steps through and you will end up with four possible ideas (at least).

IDEA GENERATOR

6. FOUR REASONS THIS WILL WORK

4. 12 WAYS IT MIGHT WORK

5. WHITTLE OUT THE RUBBISH

CHALLENGE IT: ASK QUESTIONS
Would it be better if you added something to it?
Would it be better if you took something away?
Would competitors be scared? Why wouldn't
people buy it? Is it physically possible?
Is it financially viable? Is it ownable? Is it simple?

1. What do you want to do?
   Rephrase it three times

2. How are you going to do it?
   Rephrase it three times

3. Four ways it won't work

ASK THE RIGHT QUESTION   ASK THE RIGHT QUESTION   ASK THE RIGHT QUESTION

So you've got your list.

You now need to decide what you want to focus on.

I can't help you here. This will be a combination of passion, maybe income potential, maybe ease of doing it. A simple way to look at it is to make a list of the positives and negatives of each idea. There's a template on the opposite page.

Positives | Negatives

So that's what you want to do (you may have started this book knowing that but it's good to reconfirm it).

Now, here's a good bit of advice:

Avoid all business bollocks. Words like Robust. Sustainable. Paradigm Shift. Use really simple English. Don't try and confuse people with wordy-nonsense that doesn't mean anything just because you heard it on The Apprentice. Use as few words as possible. Turn over and write your idea down in the simplest way possible.

Would your nan understand it?
Would your kids (or grandkids)
understand it? If not, do it again.

Now, I want you to draw your idea. Real or symbolic, I don't mind. Yes, it's that drawing thing again – but you don't need to be artistic. It just helps simplify your thinking.

Have you thought about what a good job looks like for you? This could be quite traditional like 'achieving a turnover of £200k by year 3' or really qualitative like 'to be known for making the longest-lasting shoes in the world'.

It's probably good to get a balance of the two.

So write down your quantitative aims and your qualitative aims to help define your vision.

What does a good job look like for you? Quantitatively (money, sales, that sort of thing).

And qualitatively (quality of life, happiness, that sort of thing).

Do these aims frighten you?
Are they ambitious enough?
Are they difficult to achieve?
If you answer 'No' to any of these
then do it again.

It's good to be scared.

Will they make you happy?

Will they make a difference?

What about skills? Do you have all the skills that you need to deliver this? I don't mean formal education.

Everyone knows that degrees don't equip us with the skills we need. What skills do you need to meet your vision, to make your product/service, to make your customers love you? Write them down in the two columns on the following page: Haves and Needs.

Haves | Needs

Consider how you are going to find these people/develop these skills.

DON'T BE AFRAID
TO EMPLOY PEOPLE
BETTER THAN YOU.

Remember people buy people.

So as Anthony Burrill says,
'Work hard and be nice to people'.

No-one likes a nasty pants.

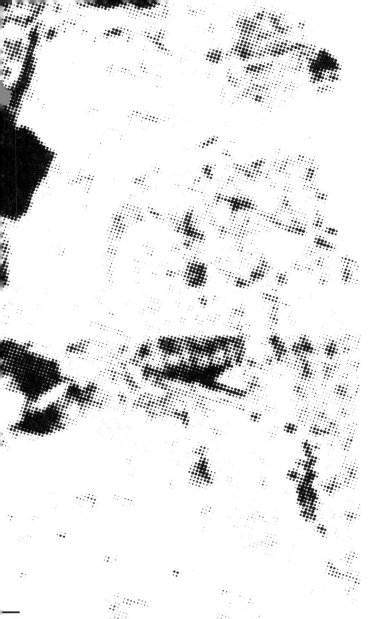

4.
THE
MARKET

So here you are. In your bedroom, shed, office, shower, with a great idea burning a hole in your head.

your
Idea

And you need to get here...

Success!

However you define it.

You need a plan of sorts, some would even call it a strategy.

Success!

Bank of Hell!

BANK

Mountains of Mayhem

Swamp of despair

Jungle of Apathy

your Idea

Strategies may sound a bit middle-management but they are useful. Honest.

You aren't going to outspend your competitors so you'll have to out-think them.

When Ben and Jerry started selling ice cream they quickly attracted the attention of a big competitor (yep, that one) who bought up all the frozen distribution in the USA which meant the boys couldn't get their lovely ice cream out of Vermont. They couldn't afford to take this company on in the courts. So they started a protest hotline (most calls between midnight and 3am), a t-shirt campaign, a radio campaign and a bus poster campaign. Guess what?

They won, the others backed down. Brains not money was the victor.

So this would be a great time to list your competitors. Remember, it's OK to like your competitors.

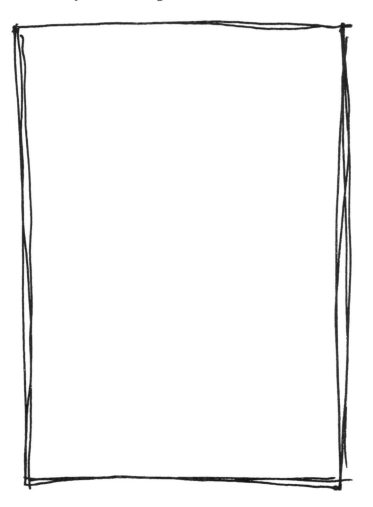

Now, what about thinking a bit broader? Think about how their product makes people feel. How else can they buy that feeling? Where from? That's also your competition. And now you've reduced the risk of missing something from left-field.

Broader competitors.

What is it you admire about your competitors?

Now think about why people might stop using the competition and start using you. What do they have to lose? What do they have to gain? Why are you knock-out?

Jerry Garcia once said,

'YOU DO NOT MERELY WANT TO BE CONSIDERED JUST THE BEST OF THE BEST. YOU WANT TO BE CONSIDERED THE ONLY ONES WHO DO WHAT YOU DO.'

List five benefits of using you.
Be specific. Be disruptive. Avoid
words like quality, value, reliable.

So, you've got a great idea. You're going to offer something different.

But to whom?

Define your customer.

You can't say 'people like me'.

That's lazy.

Who is your customer? Age? Education? Hobbies? Where do they shop? What do they do in their leisure time? What brands do they associate with? Write this stuff down in the space below.
Maybe draw another stick man.

I'm going to ask you to do some cutting and sticking now. Don't shy away from this one, it's really useful. I want you to run around the house/doctors' waiting room/newsagents and take as many magazines as you can (please pay for them first). Then I want you to cut out people, places, things, activities that relate to your customer and I want you to build a photo montage of their lives: Family, house, possessions, kids, cars, jobs, pets. Don't be shy. This helps build a detailed picture of both the customer and the context.

You won't have room to do it in this book so use a big bit of lining paper.

I've done this exercise with hundreds of clients. It's very 'Blue Peter' but after a few minutes' reticence they really get into it. There's nothing better than seeing MDs on their hands and knees cutting and sticking. There's also nothing better than going back to the client six months later and seeing the montage on the wall, still being modified, still being used.

Now, it's also worth looking at the flipside. Who is your non-customer? Who do you need to convert to buy from you? Who should want your products but doesn't know about them? Who thinks they are too young, too old, too whatever to use your products ?

List them below.

So, what are your customers really buying? That sounds crazy, huh? They'll be buying your product (hopefully) but at the moment, where are they getting the same utility, the same happiness from? It's worth thinking about this a little.

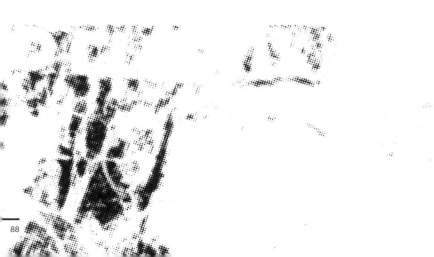

Suppose you sell bikes. People buy bikes for a number of reasons. They buy them as a leisure/sports activity, or a form of transport, or a way of losing weight/getting fit, or having time alone to think.

So as a bike seller you are also competing with exercise machines, cars, fishing rods, running shoes, meditation classes, leisure centres, and walking.

How else can your customers get
the benefits that your product or
service provides?

So what are you really selling?

What benefit are you selling ?

Your customers are exposed to really sophisticated branding.

Their expectations are high.

Remember this.

You need to be good.

YOU NEED TO BE DIFFERENT.

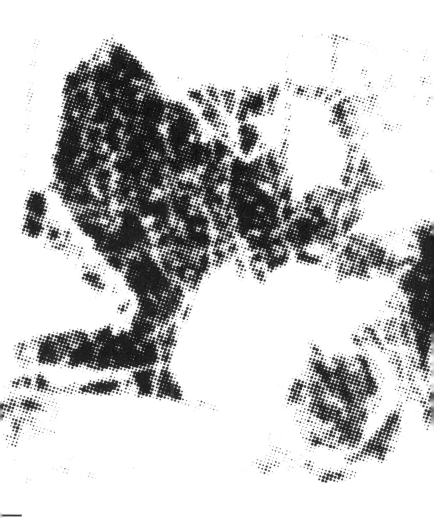

5.
INNOVATE

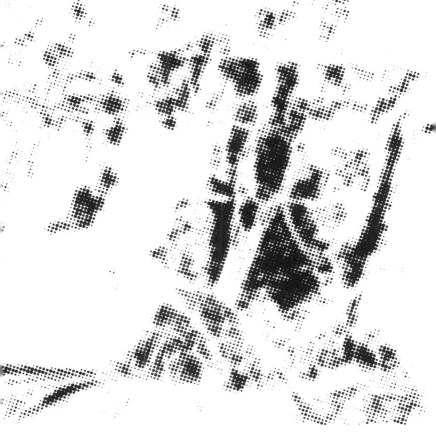

So you've identified your competition and worked out who your customer is. How will you offer them something truly different ?

What about innovating? It's really important that you continue to innovate. If you don't you'll fail. I don't necessarily mean bringing out new products. It could be just doing what you do better, in a different way. Over Christmas 2012 John Lewis saw a 44% increase in online sales. They didn't invent a new internet, they simplified, they worked out why people change their mind at the last minute, they removed navigation, they embraced mobile. Nothing revolutionary but all innovative in their own way.

And very effective.

So how do you innovate?

For some it's a natural thing, whereas others need a process in place. Innovation processes are two-a-penny.

Below is the one that I use.

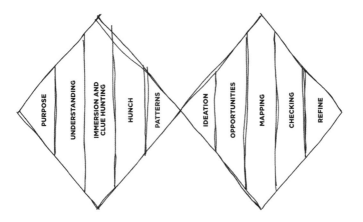

PURPOSE · UNDERSTANDING · IMMERSION AND CLUE HUNTING · HUNCH · PATTERNS · IDEATION · OPPORTUNITIES · MAPPING · CHECKING · REFINE

Start with a focused question. For example – how can we build a better table? Then go as wide as possible to understand the brief and look for clues. Be disruptive, ask things like 'why don't we all eat out of pelican bibs'. Then narrow to focus on hunches and patterns. From here, develop ideas and go as wide as possible again. These ideas generate opportunities which in turn are mapped and checked for relevance. Then the fettling and refining begins. Most innovation processes are similar. But it's not the process that delivers.

It's the people involved.

Always.

You've got to...

Keep your radar on. Always.

THE BEST INNOVATIONS SOLVE PROBLEMS THAT PEOPLE DIDN'T KNOW EXISTED.

You need to identify insights.

The challenge is to distinguish between valuable insights and value-less insights. We all spot things people are doing, but understanding which of these lead to wider-scale change and which are fads is tough.

How do you identify insights?
Where do you look? How often?
Do you use trend-spotting websites,
read contemporary journals, talk to
customers? Watch people?

Here's an example. VF (owners of Lee and Wrangler) observed that women didn't enjoy buying jeans. In fact women rated buying jeans as the second most intimidating clothes shopping experience. Cuts were confusing. Vanity sizing didn't help. Jeans were poorly displayed. VF simplified sizing and cuts, changed displays and communication, and saw a $100 million increase in revenue.

(Story from Scott Anthony's *The Little Black Book of Innovation*.)

THE SECRET IS TO PREDICT WHAT YOUR CUSTOMER WANTS BEFORE THEY KNOW. HERE'S A HANDFUL OF SIMPLE WAYS TO DO THIS.

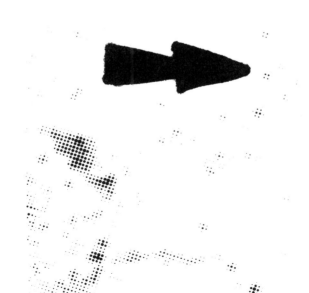

→ 1 Spend time with people to identify their problems, needs and opportunities. What need is your idea addressing?

→ 2 Watch for work-a-rounds. People will short-cut badly designed products and services and develop their own work-a-round. Spot these and BINGO!

→ 3 Focus on non-consumers. Don't restrict your thinking to your known market. There will be hundreds of people out there that love what you have to offer. They just don't know about it yet.

So how are you going to tell people about the super-duper product or service you've made?

We all know that routes to market have changed. The internet rules, yes? Well, yes that's true but the internet is a big place and you're quite small.

It can be a bit like...

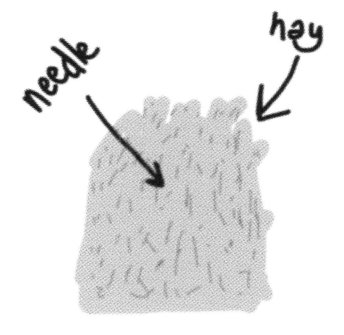

needle

hay

So you need to create a bit of a stir and build your tribe.

What are your planned routes to market? How are you going to get heard above the noise? Sometimes talking to customers in a different way is enough to get their attention. Sometimes you need to do the opposite of your competitors. Sometimes use social media, sometimes traditional media.

How are people going to find out about you? About how great you are? You don't want to keep it a secret.

6.
DETAILS

It's about time we considered the issue of money. How much do you need to generate to cover your costs? (Don't forget to include a salary for you – more common than you'd think.) How much of your product/service do you need to sell to break even? What's the profit per unit? What if costs rise? What will you do before that point? Do you need investment? If so, how much? Can you take advantage of R&D tax credits?

I know it's boring, but it's important.

Great ideas are often derailed by poor cash-flow and financial stuff.

So get it right.

Spend some time getting to grips with the numbers. But don't lose your vision, there are ways of making the numbers work if you want something bad enough.

So, now we're getting somewhere.

It's time to do a SWOT analysis. Oh great, I hear you say. A bloody SWOT analysis. Don't scoff. These things may be a bit basic but they work. So stop shirking and get the Strengths, Weaknesses, Opportunities and Threats written down. Be honest. Think about what we've looked at so far: the market, competitors, customers, cash-flow, skills (or lack of), and so on.

Strengths | Weaknesses

Opportunities | Threats

Ideally you want more things written down on the left-hand side of the page than the right. But don't be dismayed if you haven't.

For each Opportunity, Weakness and Threat I want you to write three actions.

For each Strength I want you to punch the air enthusiastically, whoop and holler – or just give yourself a little self-satisfied smile.

Action points

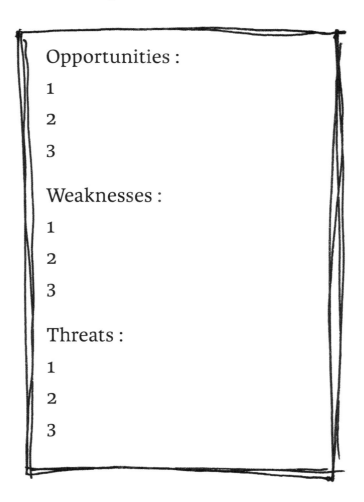

Opportunities :

1

2

3

Weaknesses :

1

2

3

Threats :

1

2

3

OK. That's all been good. All lovely and straightforward. Now I want to focus on the things that are stopping you being awesome. On the opposite page I want you to list all the things that you think stand in the way of you being brilliant.

Perceived barriers

It's dead simple.

Identify.

Remove.

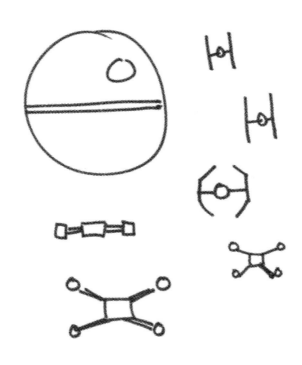

So, to summarise, you've worked out if you want to be happy, had a word with the 20-year-old you, had a chat to your Nan, done some drawing, listed your ideas, generated some ideas, measured your life with a tape measure, done some more drawing, defined what a good job looks like, defined your customer, looked at what you're really selling, written down your haves and needs, looked at insights and innovation, listed five benefits of using you, planned the routes to market, identified barriers, thought about the numbers, done a SWOT, written an action plan.

Got your head straight and resolved to start.

There is only one thing left.

GO
AND
DO.

May the force be with you.

Resources

Unboss, Lars Kolind & Jacob Bøtter, Jyllands-Postens Forlag (2012)

It's Not How Good You Are It's How Good You Want To Be, Paul Arden, Phaidon Press Ltd (2003)

S.U.M.O. (Shut Up, Move On): The Straight Talking Guide to Creating and Enjoying a Brilliant Life, Paul McGee, Capstone Publishing (2006)

The Path of the Doer, David Hieatt and Andy Smith, The Do Book Company (2010)

Consumed: How Shopping Fed the Class System, Harry Wallop, Collins (2013)

Fast Company, www.fastcompany.com

Wired, www.wired.co.uk

Trend Hunter, www.trendhunter.com

Seth Godin's Blog, http://sethgodin.typepad.com/

About the Author

Mark Shayler is a founding partner of the Do Lectures, helps run Good for Nothing, keeps chickens, ducks and children (all free-range) and runs Tickety Boo, a small innovation and environmental consultancy. He has worked with some of the world's largest and smallest businesses, saving them shed loads* of carbon, over £100 million and helping develop new products and services. He is a Virgo who will never get over failing to play professional rugby and not being the lead singer of an indie rock band. But there's still time and nothing is impossible.

* Technical term

Thanks

Thanks go to my folks who gave me a happy childhood;
my kids (Daisy, Max, Tilly and Moo) for being fantastic and
keeping me young; my Nan for still being here; and the
current Mrs Shayler for being my true love.

Thanks also to the inspirational Do community, all of you;
and my team at Tickety Boo.

Notes

Notes

Notes

Other books in the series:

Do Birth
A gentle guide to labour and childbirth
Caroline Flint

Do Disrupt
Change the status quo. Or become it
Mark Shayler

Do Grow
Start with 10 simple vegetables
Alice Holden

Do Improvise
Less push. More Pause. Better results.
A new approach to work (and life)
Robert Poynton

Do Lead
Share your vision. Inspire others.
Achieve the impossible
Les McKeown

Do Protect
Legal advice for startups
Johnathan Rees

Do Purpose
Why brands with a purpose do better
and matter more
David Hieatt

Do Sourdough
Slow bread for busy lives
Andrew Whitley

Do Story
How to tell your story so the world listens
Bobette Buster

Available in print and digital formats
from bookshops, online retailers
or via our website:
thedobook.co

To hear about events and
forthcoming titles, you can find us on
Twitter @dobookco, Facebook
or subscribe to our online newsletter.